THE ECONOMIC FUTURE

OF

THE UNITED STATES

THE FLAW

IN

LAISSEZ FAIRE CAPITALISM

Duard L Pruitt

REVISED FEBRUARY 2013

1

CONTENTS

FOREWORD

The economic future should be bright. We still inhabit a relatively prosperous country with relatively rich farm lands, a lot of economic infrastructure, and a relatively good (though not top grade) education system. Unfortunately a number of factors seem to be inexorably pulling us down. We must come to grips with all of these problems, and solve them all, to continue to be a prosperous nation.

An obvious factor that could cause ultimate catastrophe is over population. We are already overpopulated, as shown by our problems with pollution. But not yet as seriously overpopulated as most of the rest of the world. If we could somehow control our greedy and wasteful nature, control our immigration, and seriously start on the necessary job of getting out of the oil age without an economic collapse, we might still be OK. As many have pointed out, the world (and also the USA) is finite, cannot support an ever increasing population, and therefore to continue on our present course is a kind of suicide.

A more obvious and present danger are the serious flaws in our economic system (Laissez Faire Capitalism), which our ideology seems to require us to ignore, or even disbelieve. A few of us, usually university academic types, understand, and those academics have written many voluminous papers pointing out the problems. But they seem unable to get anyone to listen: most folks are still "well off" enough to just not be interested. The unemployed and seriously underemployed are less than half of the population, and that group doesn't swing many elections. Our political leaders either don't understand, or don't want to understand, or are too busy trying to get reelected that they don't seem to understand. Our political leaders are followers rather than leaders: they try to poll their constituencies to understand what they want and then cater to those wants. The wants of the wealthy are much more important than those of the poor because of the power of **MONEY** to buy influence with politicians and voters.

The basic problem is that the way laissez faire capitalism works guarantees that the rich will get richer, the poor will get poorer, and as a result we are guaranteed to have recessions and depressions. The undeniable fact that we **do have** recessions and depressions constitutes the proof that something is seriously wrong with our system.

Though not horribly complex, it does take a few words to explain, which is what I hope to accomplish in the following pages. The explanation is accompanied with an undeniable history of the great depression and World War II (WWII). This period provides all of the proof necessary, when studied carefully. Even staunch Republicans (and depression survivors) Eisenhower and Nixon were at least partial believers: their administrations at least partially preserved the New Deal tax and social structures such as social security and unemployment benefits. Serious dismantling of the New Deal/ WWII tax structure did not come until after 1980.

I. DEPRESSION HISTORY

HOW TO END A GREAT DEPRESSION

(OR HOW TO PREVENT ONE IN THE FIRST PLACE)

"A NATION THAT FORGETS ITS PAST IS DOOMED TO REPEAT IT". A quote which, in various different wordings, has been attributed to Edmund Burke (17??); George Santayana (ca 1905); Winston Churchill (19??); and possibly others.

Consider USA history during the decades of the 1920s, 1930s, and 1940s. You could hardly get more "Laissez Faire" than the 1920s, which could open a textbook case study in the shortcomings of Laissez Faire Capitalism.   Federal taxes and spending were absolutely minimal in 1929. Rules and regulations: none to speak of. The federal administrations followed a hands off policy on the economy throughout the decade. The roaring twenties ended in late 1929 with the worst financial meltdown ever, and things got steadily worse from there.   Even with the economy crashing, the administration followed a hands off policy for most of the next 3 years (taxes, including significant regressive taxes, were increased in 1932, in an attempt to balance the budget). They seemed to be waiting for private initiative to pull the country out of the depression. The depression got steadily worse.

Reference:

http://www.taxhistory.org/thp/readings.nsf/ArtWeb/1AEBAA6 8B74ABB918525750C0046BCAF?OpenDocument .

(NOTE: This URL may be obsolete. Use it as the basis of a web search.).

When the "new deal" administration took over in March 1933, there was considerable fear that the economy was about to crash completely, with resulting anarchy and chaos. To avert an imminent widespread bank failure, a bank "holiday" was declared, with some "jaw-boning" (such as "the only thing we have to fear is fear itself"). A deposit insurance law was rushed through the congress in days. The banks were reopened in groups, strongest banks first. Some job programs were instituted, to put some of the jobless back to work. An alphabet soup of new agencies were created with the objective of reviving business. The situation improved, and a certain stability returned to the country, but at a low level. As the 1930s went on, the depression stubbornly refused to go away.

Then, as the 1930s rolled along, an event happened that ended the depression very quickly: WWII started. After a brief period of complete neutrality, the US began to rearm and draft people into the military. The lid on spending disappeared, and, by 1943, nearly everybody was working. We gradually became less neutral, and then the Pearl Harbor attack propelled us completely into the war. As the war progressed, in an attempt to fund the giant war expenditures, the progressive income tax became very progressive (94% on the maximum bracket), and was extended downward to cover the whole middle class and even below. (See the history reference above.) Instead of wrecking the economy (some conservatives, and even some liberals, will maintain that high taxes will kill the economy), these measures resulted in the most efficient and productive economy the world had ever seen. Our economy was even used to rebuild Western Europe and Japan after the war.

I have had a conservative argue with me (on an internet blog) that WWII didn't start until 1941, and he felt that the depression was over in 1940, so according to him there was no correlation. But that argument is deeply flawed. First, looking at the unemployment figures, the depression wasn't completely over until about 1942, well into the war. Secondly, WWII really started to heat up in the mid 1930s, with Ethiopia, Spain, Rhineland, - - - (even in the 1920s if you count the Japanese expansion). By 1938 both the French and the British were buying war materials from us: particularly airplanes (P36s, P40s, and what became the P51), and the British also bought the obsolete General Grant tanks for use in

North Africa and bought the "more modern" General Sherman tanks when they became available. Not to mention all kinds of food, guns and ammunition, cargo ships, and even destroyers and jeep aircraft carriers (a lot of this was never paid for). And, probably with an eye on the Japanese, we had started seriously upgrading our navy by the middle 1930s, escalating toward a "two ocean navy" (ca 1940) after the German war started, and began drafting soldiers in early 1941. Our destroyers even traded shots with German submarines in the North Atlantic well before we were an official combatant. We had occupied Iceland, and were escorting cargo ships to the Iceland area well before we declared war with Germany.

To the extent that the depression was "ameliorated" between 1932 and 1940, it was due to things like the WPA and CCC and all of that mid to late 1930s war stimulus, not something magical about the business cycle. I also like to repeatedly note that, after a 1920s era of extremely low taxation (with resulting economic meltdown), income taxes were moderately high (63% max) from 1932 on, and became very high (94% max) at the peak in 1944. The lesson: The current dogma, preached by both major parties, that low taxes are necessary to escape from a recession or depression, is **sheer nonsense**! Providing full employment is the formula for ending a recession or depression. And it won't happen automatically as a result of some magical private enterprise initiative. The government(s) need to provide **a lot of stimulus** and maybe even hire people. And it should be mostly or even totally paid for by a highly progressive tax structure: personal income, business, gift, and estate taxes. And as was conclusively shown by the Great Depression / WWII history, the high taxes will not hinder economic recovery in the least.

Unfortunately, as the war came to an end in late 1945, our deep commitment to the war effort had caused us to completely forget about the deprivations of the depression, and we never bothered to analyze what it was that had caused the depression to disappear so quickly and completely. Instead, we began to dismantle the "new deal" structure almost before the last shot was fired. At first slowly, and by such means as congressmen "selling" tax avoidance provisions (loopholes) for financial support from the rich guys. Then, ca 1980, a final orgy of tax reduction and regulation repeal began that may not have ended yet. But it has already brought on some events that might seem eerily familiar if we would just study the start of the "Great Depression": Savings and Loan debacle; overheated stock market boom and subsequent decline; overheated real estate boom (bubble) and subsequent bust; giant bank failures; and now widespread lay offs. So far, the current "great recession" of 2008 doesn't appear to be nearly as bad as the 1929-1933 crash, and this may be because we haven't yet completely wrecked all of the new deal related reforms: we still have social security, medicare and medicaid, some welfare, and some unemployment benefits. Also, both major parties have participated in "bailing out" (with tax money) large firms to prevent their failure (automobiles, large New York banks). Also, there has been a small amount of "stimulus" spending.

Getting back to the "New Deal" in the early 1930s: The wealthy sector learned how to avoid the high marginal tax rates (simply "influence" your company(ies) to declare only small, if any, dividends, and retain most of the profits in what would become untaxed, "unrealized capital gains"). As a counter, Roosevelt cooked up a business tax law which, in effect, allowed distributed profits (dividends) to go essentially untaxed (as a business, or corporate, tax), but slapped a high tax rate on the "retained profits". This ploy was unpopular with the rich, and the "Conservative Coalition" of the late 1930s (Northern Republicans and Southern Democrats) was able to defeat this "retained profits" tax.

Conservatives, in general, like to blame our problems on high taxes (even when, as now (2011), taxes have been low for years), and onerous regulations. Sorry, conservatives, but that is all myth. As demonstrated by the decade of the 1920s, minimal taxation with minimal regulation is the prescription for starting a Great Depression, not ending one. As was conclusively shown by the Great Depression/ WWII experience, the truth is just the opposite:

The "New Deal" in 1933 had the correct medicine, but was too timid (or perhaps politically unable) to administer it in large enough doses. Using 20-20 hindsight, it is obvious that the onset of WWII, with the resulting full employment, high taxes, and huge spending, is what actually ended the Great Depression. As pointed out by the quotation at the top of this chapter, these are lessons that we ignore at our peril.

II. THE FLAW IN LAISSEZ FAIRE CAPITALISM

Long ago, in Medieval England, there was a mythical character named Robin Hood, who robbed the rich and gave the loot to the poor. Undoubtedly this is just a fairy story and a myth. How ironic that modern day society has developed a perfectly legal way to do just the opposite: rob the poor and middle classes and transfer the proceeds to the rich.   The mechanism that accomplishes this remarkable feat is laissez faire capitalism, particularly as it is currently practiced in the United States. You don't believe it? Just do some internet searching with regard to wealth distribution in the United States over the last few decades. It is undeniable that the very rich are getting richer and the poor are getting, at least relatively speaking, poorer. Or consider the recent bank bailout, to prevent failure of big important banks. Note that a significant part of the bailout money, a large amount of which will be extracted from low and middle class households via unfair taxation, went into multi-million dollar executive bonuses at the subject banks! The very people whose greed and incompetence caused the problem in the first place were rewarded handsomely at the expense of us dumb taxpayers!

In the real world, no two people are ever created exactly equal. Even identical twins are slightly different. It would be more accurate to maintain that all people *should have* equal rights. Over hundreds of years, people become differentiated into broad groups: a few owners, a somewhat larger middle class, and multitudes of workers. Since the "owners" keep all of the profits of any business, and have a definite bargaining advantage over the workers when it comes to wages and salaries, the owners tend to become ever wealthier while the much more numerous workers may not even maintain their living standard. By inheriting their ancestors wealth, owner families tend to persist as wealthy families for centuries. As the owner group continues to collect the lions share of the country's income, their share of the wealth also continues to concentrate in a tiny percentage of the population.

Laissez Faire Capitalism is "broken", and always has been. The proof lies in the most pressing economic problem in the United States: the repeated occurrence of recessions and even depressions, with resulting widespread unemployment, and the resulting inability of the unemployed people to care for themselves. Now, in the year 2011, we once again find ourselves mired in a "Great" recession. To the approximately 9% unemployed, many more underemployed, and the folks who have lost their homes, the situation seems intolerable.

Historically, we have been a relatively affluent country, compared to most of the rest of the world. This is because we occupy a bountiful land full of natural resources: rich farm lands and mineral resources such as coal, oil, iron ore, copper, gold, silver, etc., coupled with a relatively small population measured in people per square mile. Some of these mineral resources are now getting a bit exhausted, iron ore and oil in particular, and our problems with pollution show that our population is getting a bit too large for comfort, although still considerably less dense than some other parts of the world. We are still relatively affluent.

Our basic financial problem is that our wealth, always unequally distributed, has become extremely concentrated in a small segment of our population, especially over the last several decades. The wealthiest 1% of our households owns over 40% of the nations "investment wealth", and the wealthiest 10% of our households owns over 80% of the nations "investment wealth". In addition, our federal government tax policy gives investment income preferential tax treatment (lower rates than salaries and wages), and a lot of investment income escapes taxation altogether. Almost all (more than 80%) of the investment income automatically goes to the wealthiest 10% of households with low or even zero tax rates. The automatic result is an increase in the wealth of the wealthiest households, while the rest of the population, with little or no investment income and much lower salaries and wages, find it difficult to just "break even", and make little or no gain in wealth. It is literally true that the rich get richer and the poor get poorer. In a land of plenty, a significant portion of our population regularly goes without adequate food and shelter.

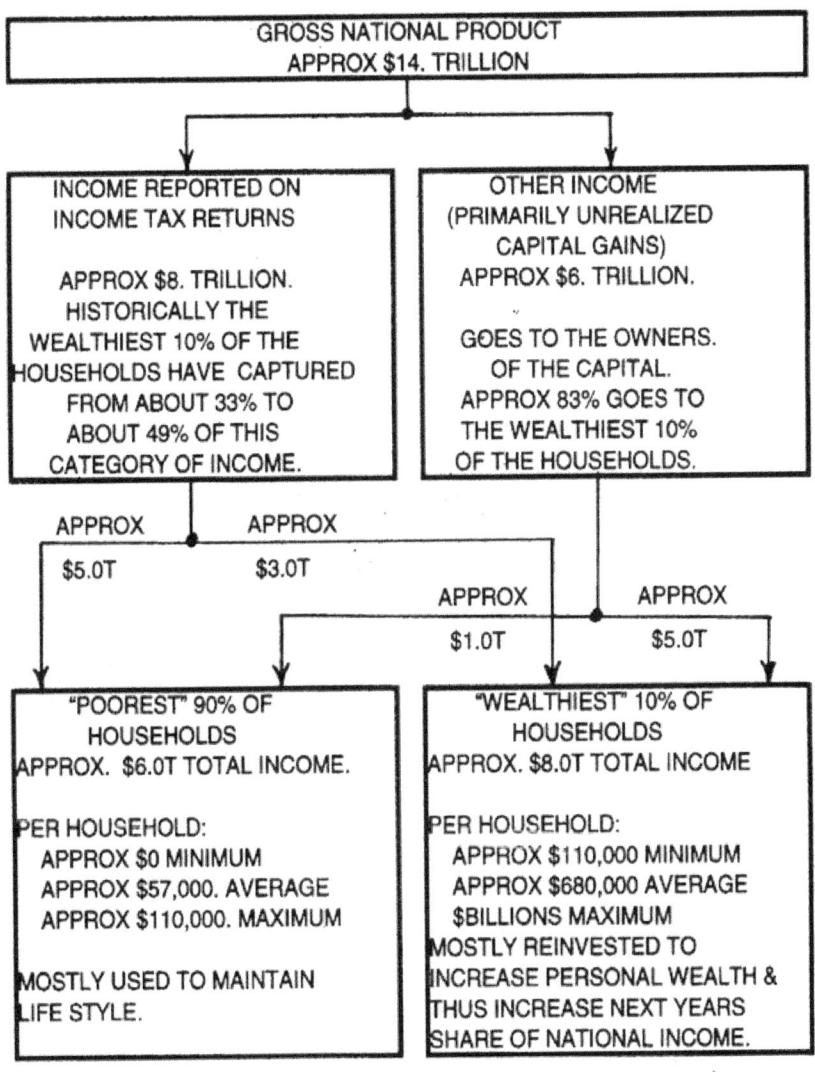

FIGURE 1. APPROXIMATE USA INCOME DISTRIBUTION

ca 2010

The state of the economy shown in Figure 1 is guaranteed by the operation of Laissez Faire Capitalism with minimal financial regulations and low taxes. The Laissez Faire system in effect operates to automatically squeeze wealth and income away from the poor and middle classes, and to automatically transfer this wealth to the ultra wealthy among us. The mechanism is brutally simple: wealthy owners have the economic power to set their own salaries (as high as their company can reasonably afford), minimize all other wages and salaries, and influence the governmental legislature(s) to write regulatory and tax laws favorable to the wealthy. Such as minimal or no regulation on economic activity, and little or no tax on investment income, and relatively low, almost non-progressive taxes on all income. As a result of low taxation, social services of course must be minimized or even eliminated (e.g., repeated attempts to repeal social security and now (2011) the brand new health care law is in the repeal "crosshairs"!).

As a result of determined application of these goals of the wealthiest households, the United States has developed an economy with an extreme concentration of the wealth of the nation in a very small percentage of the population, with resultant astronomical extremes in annual household income. Annual household income varies from virtually zero for the poorest few percent, to hundreds of millions to even billions of dollars per annum for the very wealthiest households. The entirely predictable result is a business cycle: inability of the workers and middle classes to buy all of the goods and services turned out by the economy, followed by a surplus of available goods and services, followed by business retrenchment and layoffs, which in turn worsens the initial problem and spirals into a recession or even a depression.

The "Great Recession" which we now (early 2011) find ourselves trapped in, seems to have no end in sight. Although we are a democracy, and should have the power to fix the problem by electing appropriate officials who would then fix things, we seem to keep electing legislators whose tax and social policies caused the problem, and who openly state their intention to take positions (such as repealing health care and social security laws, and further lowering taxes), which are guaranteed to make the situation worse in future years.

A part of the problem is the long "time constants" involved. From the onset of the great depression in 1929 to the onset of the great recession in 2008 was almost 80 years. It took about 25 years (from the early 1980s to about 2008) for the policies (i.e., policies that caused the great recession to occur) to take full effect, and it may take some years, even with effective recovery policies, to reverse the situation. And although the house of representatives, in principle, could be "turned around" in two years, the time constant for the Senate is much longer: six years. And the voting public doesn't have the patience to wait that long. And in the Senate a minority of 41% can prevent progress by using the filibuster technique. In addition, the opponents of reform keep up a steady stream of propaganda (paid for in large part by that wealthiest 10% and the corporations they own) to keep the voting public confused and in a state of not knowing where to turn. The result seems to be political deadlock, and things stay as they are (no reform, with even possible worsening of the problem).

We have a history of a similar problem, with similar causes, starting in 1929: the Great Depression. In that event, the situation was so bad that the voters overturned the party in power in the 1932 election. For a brief period everyone in both parties was searching for an answer and drastic changes were possible. Chaos seemed just around the corner. Over a year or two, the unemployment rate was cut from about 25% to about 15% (partly by work programs such as the WPA and CCC), lessening the worst effects of the depression, but things stalled at that point: the depression continued with high (about 10% to 15%) unemployment. Politics came back to the fore, minimizing what the administration could effectively do.

Then, something happened that almost nobody wanted, but which put everybody back on the same page and cooperating. World War II started. Fighting the war caused everybody to be put back to work (the unemployment rate fell to less than 1%). The economy was converted to war production and ran smoothly at full capacity. Money was no object, but already substantial income tax rates were raised to very high levels (by 1944) to try to minimize new debt.

Note three vital lessons here, which most of our country has yet to understand: (1) the key to ending the Great Depression was to put all of the unemployed back to work in meaningful, well paid, employment (they were, in effect, mostly working for the government, making war machines and war materials or in the armed services, but in the context of the times it was meaningful), and (2) the highest income tax rates ever <u>did not hinder</u> recovery from the depression (the myth that taxes must be low to recover from a recession or depression is just a myth: the real key is to provide full employment), and (3) the problem of the rich getting ever richer and the poor getting ever poorer was interrupted by the high progressive income tax rates. The Great Depression ended so quickly and completely that almost no one took notice. After the war, we resumed our lives as if there had never been a Great Depression, and it seems that nobody noted, analyzed, or heeded the lessons that should have been learned. All too soon, efforts were being made to undo the reforms of the "New Deal" and WWII.

Figure 2 is a graphic which shows our maximum personal income and business (corporate) profit tax rates, our unemployment figures, and some national debt history covering the time period from the early 1900s to 2010. It also shows a curve taken from an article by Piketty and Saez, the "top decile share of national income" from 1917 to 2010. To check the source of this last curve, Refer to internet URL: **http://elsa.berkeley.edu/~saez/**   and click on this item: Summary for the broader public "Striking it Richer: The Evolution of Top Incomes in the United States", updated July 2010.

These are "approximate" curves, but are accurate enough to show the correlations and prove the points to be made. Briefly, this graphic illustrates the very low personal income and business (corporate) profit tax rates of the 1920s, followed by the Great Depression starting in 1929. The moderately high income tax rates of the early 1930s are indicated, plus the very high rates of WWII

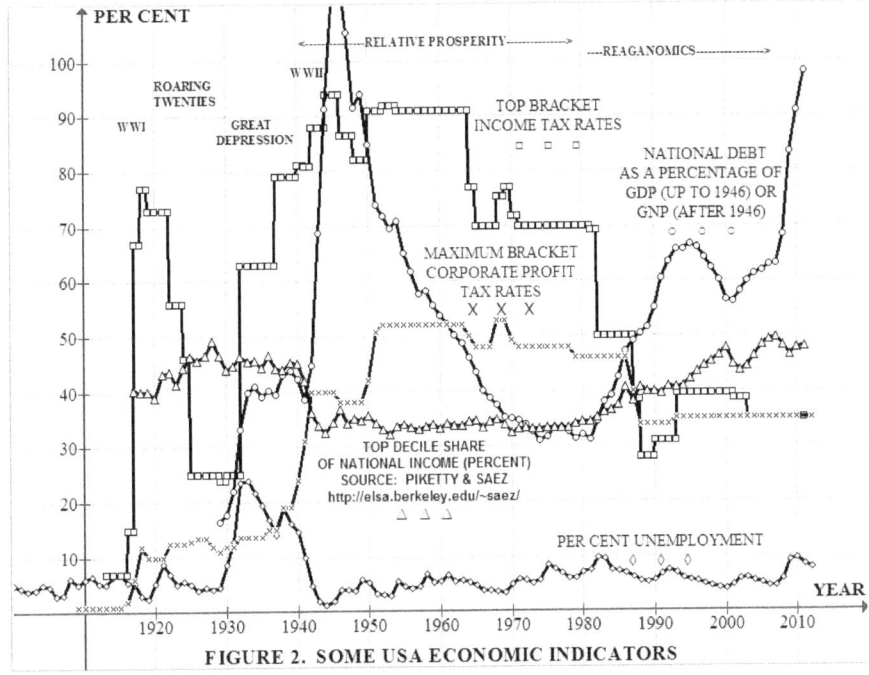

FIGURE 2. SOME USA ECONOMIC INDICATORS

which correlates with the end of the depression. It shows the relatively high income tax rates that prevailed from WWII until the early 1980s, a period of *relative* prosperity. And finally it shows the concerted push since the early 1980s (Trickle up Reaganomics) to drive tax rates down to very low levels, which culminates in the "Great Recession" of 2008. Once again, the message is clear: high progressive tax rates correlate with relative overall prosperity, and very low tax rates correlate with an oncoming recession or depression.

Study the curve of "TOP DECILE SHARE OF NATIONAL INCOME". This curve shows the portion of US income "captured" by the wealthiest 10% of the households from 1917 to 2010. Note, that during the time frame plotted, there are two high peaks in the income capture curve, denoting a capture of almost 50% of US income by this wealthiest 10% of the households: occurring in 1928 and 2007. Both of these peaks were followed by unforgettable

19

events: (1) the Great Depression in 1929, and (2) the Great Recession in 2008. Also note that for about 35 years after WWII, the amount of income captured by the wealthiest 10% stayed below about 35%, and then started a slow climb to it's 2007 peak in the early 1980s (The onset of "trickle up" Reaganomics). Reflect: it took us about 25 years (from the early 1980s) to fully develop this mess we are in now (2011).

Note the history of our national debt. We came out of the huge expenditures of WWII with a very high national debt, greater than annual GNP. After the war, the national administrations managed to steadily reduce this debt, through the Truman, Eisenhower, Kennedy, and Johnston administrations. Starting about 1965, tax reductions became a common practice. This irresponsible series of tax reductions (primarily for the wealthy), has led to a rapid increase in the national debt, since about 1980 culminating in the current recession (2011). Confirming once again that periods of low marginal tax rates are bad for the future of the economy.

Why does this happen? Basically, with their economic power, the wealthiest few per cent "hog" enough of the National income that there isn't enough left for everyone else to buy all of the products and services turned out by the economy. Instead of consuming the surplus goods themselves (basically an impossible task, given their small numbers), the wealthy invest their surplus income in an attempt to increase their personal share of the countries wealth (almost always successfully; the overall risk is small). With a resulting lack of "economic demand", production will be reduced, workers laid off, and a recession (or worse) occurs.

In recent decades, other factors have deviled the USA: production has been increasingly "outsourced" to take advantage of "cheaper labor" in other parts of the world, leading to loss of skilled jobs in the USA and a resultant "dumbing down" of the labor force into lower paying positions. Still another factor has become obvious in the current (starting 2008) recession: workers are likely to be replaced with increased mechanization and robots rather than being rehired. And guess who owns all of those robots, and economically benefits from their output? (Not the displaced workers.) These trends lead to even less demand in the USA, with further reduction in economic activity.

None of this seems to faze the "wealthy elite". In the global economy, they are quite happy to invest their surplus income wherever the return promises to be greater, even if this is in a foreign country. We are slowly drifting toward what some have called a "third world" status: an overall less skilled labor force, with under employment, unemployment, and poverty getting to be more and more the normal state of affairs for many of us, while the tiny ultra rich minority gets ever richer.

Refer to URL: **http://robertreich.org** to review a lot of observations by Robert Reich, a former secretary of labor and now a professor at the University of CA.

The prescription for a cure is fairly simple: (1) Initiate programs of social insurance (Universal Health Care, Universal Retirement Insurance [social security], and Unemployment Insurance) to mitigate the worst effects of business downturns, and (2) Pay for the insurance programs with seriously progressive income and corporate taxes (similar to WWII personal income tax), which is the topic of another chapter. To misquote a famous person, **"this could be the moral equivalent of war"**. The history of WWII says that this would be a winner. The economy would hum like a top. Step (2), of course, in conjunction with a suitably progressive estate tax, would interrupt the problem of the rich getting ever richer and the poor getting ever poorer, which would result in relative stability, as in the period following WWII.

In a separate chapter I have outlined suitably progressive income and corporate taxes (patterned after the WWII income tax structure), and shown how the system could be made self correcting, if we could just learn to keep our hands off the tax system for a while - - - (the economic time constants are *large*). Briefly, in a good economic period, when federal tax revenue exceeds expenses, **don't** lower taxes: keep hands off the progressive tax structure and pay off any national debt outstanding (once the national debt is zero, resolve to never borrow again). Any remaining surplus tax revenue should then be used to contract the currency: shred it in the treasury shredders, keeping appropriate records of course. With less money circulating (stronger dollar), prices will fall, and tax revenue will also fall, reducing the surplus tax revenue. If a business downturn should result in insufficient tax revenue, the feds should expand the currency by continuing to support and pay for all ongoing programs anyway. The federal government should **NEVER** be allowed to shut down for "lack of funds". The resulting expanded currency re-fuels the economy resulting in an increase in tax revenue and a stable economy back at square one with everybody happy! An engineer will recognize this as a **negative feedback** loop (negative feedback is necessary for stability; the positive feedback which we now regularly employ leads to instability). Note: States cannot do this; States will just have to refrain from expensive programs and live within their tax income. As a sovereign power, the federal government has an economic power that we would be wise to take advantage of to keep everyone fed, clothed, housed, medicated, and educated.

III. AN APPROPRIATE, RATIONAL, AND FAIR FIX

Figure 3 is a graph of approximate USA annual household income for 2006 and approximate household net worth for 2004 with the X axis being the household percentile and the Y axis being the plotted values in US$ on a logarithmic scale. A logarithmic Y axis is chosen because of the astronomical differences between the values for the low percentiles and the high percentiles.

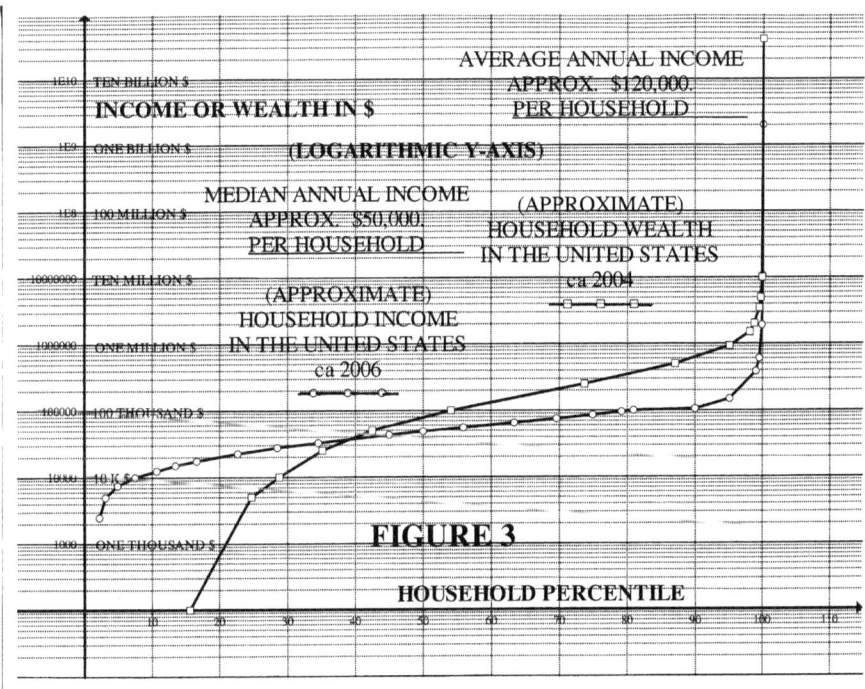

FIGURE 3

Before we analyze these curves, lets consider the estimated **approximate** cost of some basic services that every household in the country needs to obtain by some means.

In 2008, total USA health care cost:

------------ $2.3 trillion---$20,000. Per household -- 16.2% of GNP.

Source: http://www.kaiseredu.org/Issue-Modules/US-Health-Care-Costs/Background-Brief.aspx

In 2009, Social Security (retirement) cost:

------------- $0.7 trillion --- $5,900. per household ---- 4.8% of GNP.

Source: http://www.ssa.gov/OACT/TRSUM/index.html

I know, at any one time hardly more than 10% of the population (the poor retired folks, i.e., most of the retired folks) really need social security, but I will include it anyway.

Finally, unemployment insurance, a necessity for all but the ultra rich who can live solely on investment income, is more of an estimate because unemployment varies widely from year to year. More than 90% of the population needs some unemployment insurance: i.e., a guaranteed government job when all else fails. Estimated cost is based on a fairly high 7% unemployed (8 million households) and an annual cost per unemployed household of $50,000 (median household income ca 2006):

--------- $0.4 trillion --- $3,500. per household ------ 2.9% of GNP.

Please note that, from the country's point of view, these are **not** "new" expenditures. They are necessities that have to be continuously met no matter how they are paid for: whether directly from citizens pockets (or bank accounts), or from private insurance, or from government insurance, or by letting the victims starve, freeze, and die. The debate should be over the most effective and least costly (overall) method of meeting the need.

Total estimated annual cost for these three necessary items:

-------- $3.4 trillion --- $29,000. per household -----23.8% of GNP.

A comment on that final number: 23.8% of GNP for what almost everyone should agree are not only desirable, but in fact absolutely necessary services for everyone. Note that it leaves 76.2% of GNP for everything else. That is a grand total (2010 $) of about $10.9 trillion, or about $93,000 average per household, or about $35,500. average per citizen – men, women, and children – for everything else. The ultra rich would still be ultra rich, maybe just a tiny tad less so.

Now let's take a good look at Figure 3. With annual incomes less than $30,000., the poorest 30 percent of the households couldn't even think of paying that approximately $29,000. annual premium (and you could bet that any private insurance company would demand a hefty percentage of profit on top of the basic cost). And **no** private insurance company could even start to cope with unemployment insurance, with it's giant uncertainties. In fact, households out to even the 60th or 70th percentiles would have little hope of paying a $29,000. premium after meeting normal costs of living. We have to get up to a household income of $100,000. or more, before tax, (about the 80th to 90th percentiles) before you could even consider paying such a premium. **Yet the total national premium is slightly less than one quarter of total national income (before taxes and capital replacement), which is quite burdensome but also quite manageable.** This is true because of the very large incomes captured by the wealthiest 1% of the households. And that, folks, is another one of those inconvenient truths. A few thousand years ago, the tribe would have taken care of everybody in the tribe, even when it was inconvenient. Nowadays, in more civilized times, we have a very vocal minority (the ultra rich) who, in effect, seem to have convinced the voting majority to let the victims starve, freeze, and die. And the funny thing is that at least 90% (maybe as much as 98%) of those voters are potential victims themselves.

What should be done about it? WWII provided the answer, as shown previously. The required insurance programs should be provided by the Federal Government (for maximum fairness, effectiveness, uniformity of rules from place to place, country-wide availability of benefits, and minimum overall cost), and paid for by a progressive income tax structure (such as in WWII), with marginal rates up to at least 90%. All income, including all investment income, should be treated the same. No loopholes or tax shelters allowed. The system would provide catastrophe insurance for all. Once again, the 1930s and 1940s showed the way, though not all of the proposed new deal solutions (e.g., corporation tax rates) were fully approved by the Congress in the 1930s and 1940s.

How do we do it? Maybe we can't. With our legislative system, there must be at least a 61% majority in the Senate to be sure of passing reform legislation. And to achieve that super majority could take six years or more, even if the voters could be educated about the problem. The first step is to educate the nations voters as to how 90% or more are being cheated by the current Laissez Faire Capitalistic system, and to vote only for a party which pledges to fix the system by massive federal action. And the ultra wealthy would be flooding the airways with misleading (even untrue) propaganda from then on. Single minded voting for the **REFORM** party candidates for years on end (forever!) is a necessity. States can't fix the problem, and even if they could it would be inconsistent and unfair from state to state. What would you do if you became seriously ill or injured in North Carolina but your Alaska or Hawaii insurance wouldn't cover you outside of Alaska or Hawaii? (Actually, we have this problem right now: "out of network" insurance problems.) Only the federal government has the monetary power to fund and operate such an endeavor.

Trying to be as brief as possible, the required measures include the ones alluded to above: universal unemployment insurance, universal (and considerably strengthened) social security, universal health care (join the rest of the world!), and all paid for with highly progressive income and corporate taxes with no sheltered income or loopholes allowed. In addition, surplus tax revenue should be applied to pay off the public national debt, and **NO NEW PUBLIC NATIONAL DEBT TO EVER BE INCURRED AGAIN.** In the future, when tax revenue is insufficient (during a possible business recession), we make up the shortfall by borrowing from ourselves on the federal level only: expand the currency as needed, and document the expansion with special "bonds", which will be "retired" during the next prosperous period. With an expanded currency, prices will rise proportionally, everyone stays fully employed (with unemployment insurance!), and tax revenue will expand accordingly. We must **never** alter the high, progressive rate tax structure. The system described will be self regulatory and self limiting: During a prosperous period, excess revenue will, first, be used to pay off any remaining public debt, then used to upgrade and repair the national infrastructure: highways, bridges, railroads (Amtrak and other), parks, public buildings, armed services, etc., then used to contract the outstanding currency. Unemployment insurance can put the unemployed to work on such projects. And did you notice that unemployment insurance, the cheapest of the three insurance programs (less than 3% of GNP most years), is the key to preventing human suffering because of a recession? But, of course, all of the components of reform are necessary for long term stability, including permanent tax reform.

If a business downturn should result in a tax revenue shortage, we continue to pay all of our government obligations and "borrow from ourselves" as described above to prevent unemployment or any other catastrophic results from the downturn. Thus providing for quick recovery and a long term stable economy. The ultra wealthy will still be ultra wealthy, and will even continue to get wealthier (though perhaps slower than in the past). The high rates on the maximum marginal personal and corporate income tax brackets places a "partial cap" on astronomically high incomes. And a suitably progressive estate tax will provide for a partial "system reset" once per generation. To make all of this work, of course, will require absolute elimination of all tax shelters and loopholes, and eternal vigilance.

IV.   REQUIRED TAX STRUCTURE

(SIMILAR TO THE RATES FROM WWII TO THE EARLY 1960s)

A.   RULES FOR A RATIONAL, SIMPLE, FAIR, PERSONAL INCOME TAX.   BUSINESS TAX WOULD BE MORE COMPLEX; BUT BUSINESS PRINCIPAL OR INCOME PAYED OR OTHERWISE DIVERTED TO AN INDIVIDUAL BECOMES A PART OF THAT INDIVIDUAL'S PERSONAL INCOME IN THE YEAR THAT IT IS SO DIVERTED.

FEDERAL INCOME TAX FORM

(Add Personal ID information here)

1. Summary of **absolutely all** income-----_____

2. Social Security Tax. 5% of line one.---_____

3. Subtract line 2 from line 1---------------_____

4. Health Insurance Tax. 5% of line one. _____

5. Subtract line 4 from line 3---------------_____

6. IRA Deduction (maximum to be $5,000.00 per taxpayer) --_____

(NOTE: LINE 6 CANNOT BE MORE THAN LINE 5)

7. Subtract line 6 from line 5---------------_____

(NOTE: LINE 7 CANNOT BE LESS THAN ZERO)

8. Standard Deduction (see note 2)--------_____

9. Subtract line 8 from line 7 (Taxable Income) --_____

10. Tax on line 9 (see note 1)---------------_____

11. Add lines 2, 4, and 10 (total tax)------- _____

12. Estimated tax paid during the year----- _____

13. Subtract line 12 from line 11----------- _____

14. Penalty for underpayment of Estimated Tax (see note 3)
-- _____

15. Add lines 13 and 14. TAX DUE------ _____

Note 1: Tax table for line 9:

Single Filer	Rate
Any negative amount	-50% (refund)
0 to $20,000.	10%
$20,000. to $40,000.	20% + $2,000.
$40,000. to $100,000.	30% + $6,000.
$100,000. to $300,000.	40% + $24,000.
$300,000. to $1,000,000.	50% + $104,000.
$1,000,000. to $5,000,000.	60% + $454,000.
$5,000,000. to $15,000,000.	70% + $2,854,000.
$15,000,000. to $50,000,000.	80% + $9,854,000.
All over $50,000,000.	90% + $37,854,000.

Joint filers & Head of Household	Rate
Any negative amount	-50% (refund)
0 to $30,000.	10%

$30,000. to $60,000.	20% + $3,000.
$60,000. to $150,000.	30% + $9,000.
$150,000. to $400,000.	40% + $36,000.
$400,000. to $1,000,000.	50% + $136,000.
$1,000,000. to $5,000,000.	60% + $436,000.
$5,000,000. to $15,000,000.	70% + $2,836,000.
$15,000,000. to $50,000,000.	80% + $9,836,000.
All over $50,000,000.	90% + $37,836,000.

Note 2: Standard (& only allowable) deduction: $17,500. for individual; $35,000. for married filing jointly and head of household. Y2010 dollars, adjusted annually for inflation.

Note 3:   (see separate instruction, to be developed)

Note 4: There will be back up forms, of course, for listing income sources and providing for income averaging where appropriate. The primary form will be only one sheet. Notes and regulations will have to be comprehensive, to prevent any cheating or hiding of income (**NO** income sheltering allowed).

Also: All states should be strongly encouraged to start with the Federal Taxable Income when assessing their state personal income tax, to reduce paperwork and make taxation more equitable.

Also: To accommodate taxpayers who may have widely different incomes from one year to the next (e.g., sports figures, movie stars, politicians), a five year averaging should be allowed, except that the full tax due for one year averaging must be paid in year one; then use two year averaging for year two with a refund possibly due; use three year averaging for year three with a refund possibly due; etc. After 5 years have passed, drop the first year from further 5 year averaging, etc.

Also: After possible transition periods, everyone (including congressmen, teachers, etc.) must participate in social security as a primary retirement program and have health insurance coverage. The social security tax paid should be set at about 5%, and the retirement benefits paid should be calculated from the actual amount of individual payments. Extra funds which **may be required** to be made up from general tax revenue, with no penalties or recriminations for individual retirees. Likewise, the health insurance tax should be set at about 5%, with the extra that **will be required** to be paid from the general tax revenue.

Payment of the negative income tax should be coordinated with Unemployment Insurance, through the use of local Federal Unemployment Insurance offices, which could be combined with welfare offices, food stamp distribution, etc. The employers of part time and underemployed (low paid) employees would be required to collect payroll taxes and furnish the appropriate unemployment office (and/or the IRS, as appropriate) with the tax money and appropriate monthly paperwork confirming the employee's status, hours, and pay. The office would use this information and the employee's application information to figure the monthly payment due, if any, and to issue the appropriate checks to the individual employees on a current and monthly basis. An income tax return would be due at the close of each tax year, as usual, to add any outstanding income and confirm the final annual status. Each employee would be responsible for keeping the IRS and the local unemployment office updated on any otherwise unreported income, paying any estimated tax payments that might be required, and filing a regular income tax return at the end of each tax year. For cases where no local private job can be found, the unemployed person could be employed directly on some Federal Government job: such as Public building repair or construction, Amtrak upgrade or maintenance, a job related to the armed services, or national security, or perhaps for an employer who is working on a suitable government job. As a last resort, the unemployed person will receive the calculated value of negative income tax, paid and reviewed monthly.

Taxpayers may take the IRA deduction only for actual IRA contributions made to a qualified IRA custodian, and line 7 cannot be a negative amount.

B.   CORPORATE OR OTHER BUSINESS TAX

    1. BALANCE SHEET BOTTOM LINE,
        TOTAL PROFITS:--------------------_____

    2. TOTAL OF DISTRIBUTIONS
        TO OWNERS: ----------------------_____

    3. SUBTRACT LINE 2 FROM LINE 1,

        TAXABLE PROFITS:--------------_____ ____

    4. BASE TAX   50% OF LINE 3: -----------_____

    5. STANDARD DEDUCTION: ------------$100,000,000.

    6. SUBTRACT LINE 5 FROM LINE 3,

    (IF LESS THAN ZERO, ENTER ZERO)

    7. SUR TAX   30% OF LINE 6: --------------_____

    8. TOTAL TAX = LINE 4 + LINE 7: -------_____

A quick note on corporate or business tax. In recent years, our corporations have become very adept at avoiding taxation (legal evasion). With a nominal rate of 35% on profits, the amount actually paid has apparently been less than 5% of profits some years! It is high time for this to be changed, considering the immorality of the whole situation, and the need for national revenue. We need clear and simple business tax laws. No evasion or loopholes provided or allowed: all businesses must pay the required rate on all profits that are not distributed to the owners via dividends or other methods. The distributed profits should not be taxed to the corporations, to avoid "double taxation", but will be taxed as a part of the owners income. The "retained profits" should be taxed at a rate of at least 50% (higher for extremely large profit brackets). As with the personal income tax, a substantial tax rate will not in the least hinder business operations. The key is to keep the workers all employed, so that they can buy the products and keep the economy running. Exhausted or used up capital is replaced, as always, as a business expense, before declaring profits. So there is no problem with keeping the economic machine running. "Growth" is actually not even possible in the long run, because the earth (and also the USA) is finite. A very small percentage of "new investment" causes things to double in a remarkably short time, historically speaking: for example, a 1% per year NEW investment, by the workings of compound interest, causes a doubling of capital in about 72 years. Which is way too often for the country's population and infrastructure to be doubling anyway. This small (in percentage) NEW investment should be supplied from after tax income.

C.   ESTATE TAX

   1. TOTAL ESTATE VALUE--------------- _____

   2. STANDARD DEDUCTION---------- $20,000,000.

   3. SUBTRACT LINE 2 FROM LINE 1

       TAXABLE ESTATE------------------- _____

34

(IF LINE 3 IS LESS THAN ZERO, ENTER ZERO)

4. TAX ON LINE 3. SEE RATE TABLE _____

ESTATE TAX RATES: 0 TO $100,000,000.   35%

ALL OVER $100,000,000.   70%

D.   GIFT TAX

1. GIFTS UP TO $25,000. PER ANNUM, PER DONOR, PER DONEE ARE TAX FREE.

2. AMOUNTS IN EXCESS OF $25,000. PER ANNUM ARE TAXED, PAYABLE BY THE DONOR AT THE TIME OF THE GIFT, AT INCOME TAX RATES FOR A SINGLE FILER, AS IN NOTE 1 ABOVE.

What would this look like if implemented? Figure 4 shows a graph of USA household income, ca 2006, before and after taxes, with income tax assessed as proposed in the discussion just above. The declared income is shown, vs household percentile, in the "income" curve, and the household after tax income, is shown vs household percentile in the "after tax income" curve. Note that the most obvious difference in the two curves is in the low income range: though still poverty cases, the very lowest income "taxpayers" would now have a monthly income to help pay for food and shelter. At the multi-millionaire end of the curve, the after tax income is a bit less to be sure, but hardly noticeable on the logarithmic curve. They are still multi-millionaires, and the after tax line still curves upward steeply as the 100th percentile is approached, similar to the before tax income curve. NOTE: This graph does not show households above 99.99%, because of lack of data. The wealthiest

35

11,000 households have absolutely astronomical incomes, extending into the billions of dollars for the last few households just below the 100th percentile.

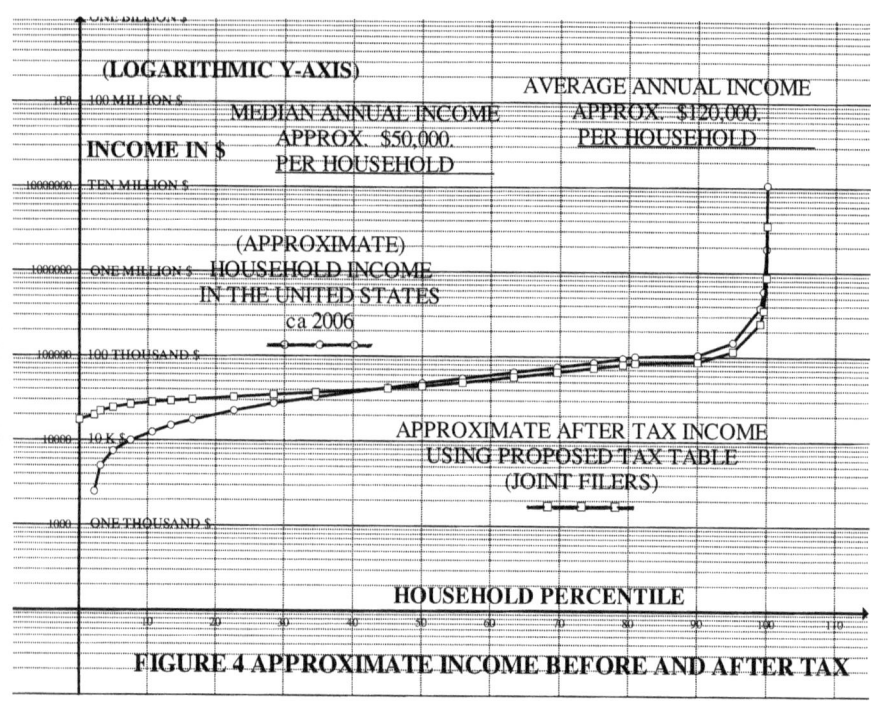

FIGURE 4 APPROXIMATE INCOME BEFORE AND AFTER TAX

V. THE CHANCE FOR REFORM

Who constitutes the worker class, and who is the owner class, anyway? In actual practice, there is no clear dividing line: the curve from minimum to maximum income is smooth, with no particular breaks. It does curve up steeply and exponentially, however, as we approach the maximum income. Some statistics tell the tale:

The lower 80% of households own about 15% of total wealth (including housing) and collect about one third of the total national income. The upper 20% of the households own the remaining 85% of the wealth and collect about two thirds of the income.

If you confine your attention to *financial* or *investment* wealth (less housing and personal wealth, which earns no profits), The upper 10% of the households own over 80% of the investment wealth. The upper 1% of the households own more than 40% of the investment wealth.

Now you know why investment income receives serious (and unfair!) tax breaks. It is because the multi-millionaires want it that way, and have the money (and power) to influence the congress to keep it that way. In a rational society, investment income would get **NO** tax breaks, and excessively high income brackets would attract excessively high tax rates to match. Several years ago the media reported that a famous billionaire called attention to this unfair difference in the way small and large incomes are taxed by pointing out that his secretary, with a **much** smaller income, paid a significantly higher overall tax rate than he himself did.

Now you are starting to get the picture. The *worker* class constitutes at least the lower income 80% of the households, probably the lower 90%, and possibly the lower 98%! The real *owner* class is confined to the top two percentiles (or maybe even just the top 1%)!

OK, now that you understand what we are up against, let us start a new political movement, dedicated to fixing the capitalistic system in the USA to prevent recessions and depressions and give everybody a fair slice of the pie. The new (or reformed) party should control congress by about 80% to 20%. Financial reform measures should sail through the congress without serious opposition. Alternate: No new party at all. Just educate, infiltrate, take over, and reform one of the existing major parties.

> No more worries that a severe illness can send your family to the poor house.

> No more worries that unemployment might do the same.

> And No more worries that you will be destitute in your old age.

So get busy. The first step is to educate that 80% - - - or 90% - - - or maybe even 98% - - ------ of the voters as to how they have been and are being economically mislead and misused, and explain what is actually happening to them. And the fact that it could be fixed by just voting for congressional candidates with the correct set of economic ideals.

In United States elections, turnout has been typically low, even *atrociously* so. In recent presidential year elections, turnout has typically been a little over 50% of qualified voters, seldom over 60%. In *off year* national elections, it is typically even lower, and in the primaries it is typically atrociously low. Observers have noticed that *heavy* turnout tends to favor the *liberals*, and conversely *light* turnout tends to favor the *conservatives*. How do we get better (higher turnout) participation in elections? I would suggest making national election days one day holidays, dedicated to going to the polls, period. Election day should be in the middle of the week to minimize using the holiday for just another day off (Wednesday would be even better than the traditional Tuesday). The traditional early November is a good time because the weather usually isn't too bad, and it is not a traditional vacation season. Maybe we could suggest that a voter get up early, go right to the polls, then go fishing. OK, Congressmen, get busy and declare national election days to be national holidays, starting right now! No one should object, since everybody at least pays lip service to the ideal of universal voting.

What are the chances of getting a workable reform majority in Congress? Probably not too good. We are just affluent enough that most voters just don't worry about financial policy and just don't understand how badly they are being treated economically, and how unstable our financial system is. Nor the manner in which the "conservative" agenda causes the recurrent recessions, depressions, and resulting unemployment and under employment. And almost everyone is caught up in what I call the "fringe" issues. Don't get me wrong, I understand that the fringe issues are important. They are even important to me, though I consider financial policy to be the number one concern. Its just that finances are so much more important to an individuals everyday welfare that he or she should never lose sight of how the candidates stand on financial policy. Since the figures from intelligent and professional University professors clearly show that at least 90% of our population should be financial "liberals", it seems fantastic that our Congress should always come out so close to a 50/50 division on financial issues: this definitely does not reflect the interests of the country. As I pointed out somewhere else, that 50/50 division translates into no change: it takes an **over** 60% super majority in the Senate to pass any contested legislation. There is really no reason for a moral financial policy to have any conflict with any of the "fringe" issues. The message: try to support a candidate who agrees with your views on most of the "fringe" issues, but by all means make sure that he (or she) also agrees with "liberal" financial policy. The place to hash this out is in the primaries: participate in the procedures as much as possible to ensure that your candidate agrees with both "liberal" finances and your most important "fringe" issues. I am talking about things like abortion, death penalty, drug policy, environment, family values, gay rights, gun control, immigration, law and order, pollution, religious tolerance, wild life, and more. (I tried to put them in alphabetical order to avoid revealing a bias). It is hard, maybe impossible, to find a candidate who is in 100%

agreement with yourself, but the place to search is in the primaries, and make financial policy the #1 priority. At this point in time, this important issue (financial policy) has been hijacked by the Conservatives, and I am at a loss to explain how they did it, unless it was just by throwing money into attack ads and emphasizing the fringe issues. They certainly did not do it with a reasonable and honest debate on financial policy.

As someone has noted, maybe in jest, things may have to get a lot worse before the voters wake up and vote to make them better. I am just afraid that he or she may be right. As I showed in the statistics presented in the earlier chapters, the policies being pushed by the new majority in the house of representatives are guaranteed to make things a lot worse over a period of a few years. Lower and lower taxes and less and less regulations are the "remedy" that has been applied since the early 1980s, and the result is the mess we are in now (early 2011). This "conservative" policy just increases the speed at which the super wealthy soak up the countries wealth and income, and hastens the advent of another year of violent recession. It really does nothing to reduce unemployment, which is the part of the recession that hurts ordinary people. In the current "2008 recession", as of 2011 the business community thinks that the recession is over (manufacturing output and profits are back up), but the people who were laid off are still, for the most part, unemployed. The workers were apparently mostly replaced by more automation and mechanization, which, of course, is wholly owned by the "owners". The outcome of the recession is thus to put the "owners" a tiny bit closer to their ultimate goal of owning almost everything, and thus capturing almost all of the national income.

VI. FORECAST FOR 2016

(WHEN THINGS WILL LIKELY BE PRETTY BAD)

What can we possibly do about Great Depression #2? The conservative policies (over the past six years) of reducing taxes to near zero, and minimizing social services and unemployment benefits, has, as should have been predicted, failed. The traditional policy of GREED as the sole remedy, has, as should have been predicted, failed. More workers have become unemployed and underemployed and remain so for the same old reason: the extreme concentration of wealth and income, which has only gotten more extreme in the last six years, prevents the operation of a true mass consumer market in the USA. There is no motive to hire more workers and produce more consumer goods: our under paid and underemployed workers cannot buy all of the goods and services that our economy is capable of turning out now. We are rapidly approaching third world status.

Unfortunately, with the current Conservative majority in Congress, and given their refusal to even consider the twin reforms of very high progressive taxation coupled with extensive social programs (Universal Health Care, Improved Social Security, a Negative Income Tax, and Public Programs to reemploy the idled workers), reform is still years away. Even if we could convince the voters to start voting overwhelmingly for reform, it would probably still take at least six years to obtain a workable Senate majority (a 41% minority can block all progress via filibuster). So things are very likely to get worse before they get better. Even if the administration relents and enacts some reform, it will likely be a minimal program intended to deflect criticism and retain power, rather than really go all out to solve the problem.

What is the problem? Our basic national economic system, commonly called Capitalism, more accurately called Laissez Faire Capitalism, has a basic flaw: it is very unstable. It legally and

41

naturally operates (over a number of years) to concentrate wealth and income in a small percentage of the population (the owners), gradually but steadily extracting said wealth and income from all the rest of us. The natural result is inability of the overall population to buy the articles and services turned out by their labor (or by the machines and robots increasingly used to replace their labor), resulting in recurrent business recessions and gradual reduction of the standard of living for the majority of the population, with a growing percentage of unemployed and underemployed. That small ultra wealthy minority seems to have the economic power to mislead and control the majority, electing legislators who are pledged to keep things just as they are: minimal taxes, minimal social services, minimal regulations, and zero reform.

How could it be fixed? It is possible to contrive an economic system, with what an engineer would call "negative feedback", a system which is self correcting under changing conditions, a system which is stable under all conditions, and a system that takes the worry and uncertainty out of all of our lives. It can be achieved by adequate social insurance programs, with high "progressive" no-loophole, no special privilege, taxation to pay the necessary premiums (the necessary national cost). To achieve the required negative feedback, the maximum marginal tax rate must be in the order of 90%, with all personal and corporate income subject to tax: no sheltered or special rate types of income to be allowed. Investment income is just the same as any other income. All tax free bonds should be retired as soon as possible and forbidden in the future. Business tax should be *zero on distributed profits*, and at least 50% on retained profits (greater than 50% on extremely large profits). The estate tax should have a very generous "deduction" (perhaps ten million dollars or even more) coupled with a very progressive rate structure with high maximum rates. The income tax should have an identical, fixed, generous standard deduction for each taxpayer with no other deductions allowed. And there is to be no tinkering with the tax structure through good times and bad, in order to achieve the "negative feedback", which stabilizes the economic system.

The negative feedback works as follows: in "bust" times (which is where we are now), extra money is fed into the system via public works programs (e.g., enhance the national transportation, energy, and other infrastructures), to keep **all** workers working and supporting themselves and their families. There should also be such things as a "negative" income tax and unemployment insurance to assist low paid and unemployed workers. The required money is not borrowed from the private sector (or other countries). The needed funds are obtained by expanding the currency (i.e., borrowing from ourselves) and keeping special bonds (similar to the present social security funding system) to document the expansion. This economic activity will revive the economy, expand tax revenues, and end the depression.

For proof that this is so, just examine the economic history of the "roaring 1920s", the "Great Depression", and World War II: by doing something very similar to the above suggestions (economically speaking) at the start of WWII, we terminated the Great Depression so completely and quickly that nobody noticed. Almost everybody was put to work doing something considered important, and the maximum marginal income tax rate was 94% in 1944. Contrary to current dogma, the high marginal tax rates **did not hinder recovery from the depression at all.**

As the "bust" period transitions into a "boom" period, we hasten to - - - do nothing! Leave the tax rates alone. There will now be an excess of tax proceeds, which will be used to retire all national debt, (so we can stop paying interest on it), and then the "paper" debt that we borrowed from ourselves to escape from the "bust" period. Any excess over these requirements will be used to "contract" the currency: shred it in the treasury shredders, keeping appropriate records of course. Once the national debt is completely retired, we never issue public debt bonds (or other debt instruments) again; just expand the currency if and as needed during any slow periods.

As noted above, an engineer will immediately recognize this financial system as being a self correcting "negative feedback" system.

43

VII. POSSIBLE PROBLEMS

Idle hands are the Devil's workshop (old saying). Since the dawn of civilization, human leaders, from tribal chiefs to emperors and dictators, have used the "surplus" fruits of capitalism to mount wars of conquest and expansion. The objective of course was to enlarge and glorify their territory (and also themselves). The chief (or king or dictator) used the "surplus" labor to build castles and towns, ships and chariots, and outfit armies and navies. This had the good effect that it kept all of the citizens occupied: employed, fed, clothed, and housed (if they were on the winning side). It also had the bad effect that it caused an awful lot of human misery (especially if you were on the losing side). The King or Queen typically used divine right as the excuse for appropriating the extra resources for the state.

For thousands of years, there wasn't much surplus: most of a population were farmers and only a few per cent lived in cities. For many thousands of years world human population grew slowly. In extreme ancient times, it took 2,000 years or more for the population to double. In the Roman era, it took about 500 years for the population to double. A wikipedia article indicates that as late as 1800 the percentage of population living in cities was only about 3%, and total world population in 1800 was a little less than one billion. With the dawn of the industrial revolution in the late 1700s, output per man hour started to increase dramatically, enabling a faster increase in world population. This increase accelerated dramatically starting in the late 1800s with the dawn of the petroleum (or oil) age. At its peak of growth, the world population doubled in about 40 years. As of 2011, the world population is estimated at nearly seven billion. Most of these 7 billions have appeared on the scene in about the last 150 years, during the oil age. Now, more than half of us live in cities, and the farmers constitute a small percentage of the total population, at least in industrialized countries. Power and fertilizers (both derived primarily from petroleum and related minerals) have enabled us to produce seven times (or more) as much food as we could produce 200 years ago.

Now we are living at the peak of the oil age, and the most optimistic projections are that resource depletion will essentially end the oil age in a matter of decades (not hundreds of years).

What will replace the oil age? We really don't know. Electricity from various "renewable" sources is a dim possibility, but electricity is tied mostly to wires and may not be suitable for tilling the farm fields. Bio fuels are a possibility, but to produce them in any quantity would require diverting agricultural resources from food production, which is sorely needed to feed those seven billion people. But if we don't come up with some kind of fuel for the tractors, and some kind of fertilizer for the fields, the food production will fall anyway. Going back to horses and oxen is not an option: that is what we used for thousands of years and the overall "efficiency" was low, limiting us to smaller populations.

There is another factor at work that is biting us now: mechanization, automation, and robot usage is increasing relentlessly, improving "efficiency" and increasing production with many fewer workers required. The displaced workers don't own the machinery that replaced them, so don't participate in the profits. Without a job and with few possessions, the workers are destitute. Thus, they (the displaced workers) can hardly feed themselves, and can't buy any of the marvelous things made by the automated machines. The long term outcome of this situation is already clear: a large percentage of poverty class citizens, a very small percentage of super wealthy owners, and a smaller "middle class" - - - in short, what we now call a "third world" country. Will this be a "paradise" for the super wealthy? Don't bet on it. Remember, idle hands are the Devil's workshop. The idle, and poverty stricken, "workers" aren't likely to go quietly. Drug use and crime are likely to become rampant. At some point, riots are a possibility: I understand that one of the problems in the Egypt of 2011 is an unemployment rate on the order of 25%, which is about the same rate that almost caused havoc early in our Great Depression.

This is a real quandary. As pointed out in the earlier chapters, given the political will, we could easily cure the economic flaws in our society today. But in the brave new world where machines and robots do most of the work, providing the workers with scads of leisure time, what to do with that time could turn into a problem. People seem to be "itchy": if they aren't busy doing something worthwhile they get into trouble. One theory says that is our drug problem of today. Too many idle youths form unwholesome gangs and "do drugs", among other things. I will admit that I don't have a pat answer, and that this potential problem merits a lot of study.

In the short term, we need to provide useful jobs for all of the "displaced" workers. An effective border patrol, to control immigration, could actually employee millions of people. Upgrading Amtrak (to a high speed country wide network) and upgrading infrastructure in general could employee additional millions. Building and operating a "green" energy establishment is another opportunity for employing millions of otherwise unemployed. We have to do what we can, keep the workforce employed, and move into the future one step at a time.

VIII. PARADISE

(EXTRA CHAPTER)

A paradise land in the United States would be far in the future, if at all. Almost by definition, a true paradise is not achievable on Earth. Maybe exaggerating a bit, I would define paradise as a USA of the distant future with a stable population of no more than 200 to 300 million people. Since earthly mineral resources would be all but completely depleted by this time, this population would have to live a much calmer life than we typically indulge in now. Recycling of virtually all materials would be absolutely required. This population would live mostly in the cities, since personal transportation is expensive. I would envision "town house" like rows of homes, with most homes being 20 to 30 feet wide by 50 to 60 feet deep, joined together in row house fashion to conserve energy, with outdoor living space on the roofs and maybe provision for moving from roof to roof. Little or no outside yard space for these houses. A ground level garage would house a smallish electric vehicle which "plugs in" to a house electrical outlet when not in use. This vehicle would be limited to a radius of perhaps 25 to 50 miles (to save on battery volume and cost), and would provide local transportation only. The city would have the usual metropolitan public transportation systems, electrified rail, bus, and subway lines. A network of high speed electrically powered trains would provide city to city transportation, with connections to things like national parks. Air transportation would have to be greatly reduced and used only for very important things like emergencies, because of the shortage of suitable fuels. Overseas travel would not be as commonplace as it now is, because of the expense. Fabulous vacations would be by train, maybe renting an electric vehicle at the destination.

To compensate for this relative lack of mobility, the insides of these town houses would be absolutely luxurious, with the latest in high definition and 3D televisions, high quality sound systems, and computer terminals. The cities would have movie theaters, of course, and medium to larger cities would have orchestras with symphony halls and other entertainment centers. Sports of all kinds would still be common. The sports teams would have to resort to the high speed rail system to travel, just as their counterparts of the early 1900s traveled by *lower speed* trains. Residents, with more spare time now in the age of automation, may spend more time in parks, museums, and sports centers. "Intramural" sports and games could be organized to provide some friendly competition between city neighborhoods.

The factories would be highly automated, with extreme efficiency in terms of output per person-hour of labor. The modified capitalistic economy, discussed earlier in this book, would have solved the resulting compensation problems long ago. People would work fewer hours per week, with more days off, and compensation per hour or per day would be much higher than it would ever have been under Laissez Faire Capitalism. Fuel and material shortages and resulting premium transportation costs have greatly curtailed the once mighty "global economy". Food and manufactured goods now have to be produced much closer to the point of use: routinely transporting items thousands of miles is no longer an option economically. The transportation problem will limit the size of the cities: huge cities would require too much surrounding land to supply them with food, in turn requiring excessive transportation costs. Conversely, tiny towns would be rare also: the city needs to be large enough to supply most required services and products locally, to minimize transportation costs. Workers in the new cities would travel to work within their city via the city electrified transportation network. Some may work at home via computer terminals. Most food would be locally grown (within dozens or hundreds rather than thousands of miles). Likewise, with automated factories everywhere, and prohibitive transportation costs, there is no advantage to foreign sourcing of most goods. All manufactured items will be designed for easy maintenance, and for complete recycling.

The electrical power industry will have been gradually "weaned off" of fossil fuels and on to renewable sources such as sunlight, wind, water (river and tidal power), geo thermal, "bio", etc. Nearly all national power, including transportation, will be derived from the AC electrical power grid.

Everything, including especially the housing, will be designed and constructed for long life and ease of maintenance. Buildings and cities will be located to avoid natural hazards such as flood prone and land slide prone areas. The buildings will be designed to withstand severe weather, and, insofar as practical, earthquakes.

IX POST SCRIPT

SAVING

Save for a rainy day. Saving for future needs is an admirable part of human activity. But, as with most things, there are some limitations.

If we are trying to save physical objects, we have to be aware that they can deteriorate with time. Food spoils quickly unless "preserved", dried, or frozen, and even then it won't "keep" indefinitely --- maybe a year or so at most for most foods. Dried grains may last several years, if we can protect them from mice and rats. Pictures fade, musical records and DVDs deteriorate over the years and even become unusable. Cars, TVs, and even production machinery can become "obsolete" with time, as well as corroding away. Clothes go out of style.

Ah, but we can save our money, can't we, and just buy new stuff when we are ready? Yes, to a certain extent, but reflect that this only works because there are millions of us out there; most of us spend most if not all of our money every month to maintain our standard of living; we don't all decide to save up a lot of money each year, and over a few years time most of us spend most of our money anyway, savings and all. It all tends to even out over the 300 million population. A glaring exception are the ultra rich among us, who save (and reinvest) most of their incomes each year. All, or essentially all, of the products and services produced this year have to be sold this year, or they will start to deteriorate, and the retail business establishments will be in trouble financially. In fact, the trigger for a recession or depression is a drop in retail sales when the general population runs short of spending money. For the economy to run smoothly, nearly all of the goods and services produced this year must be consumed this year. If sales falter, inventories build, factories slow down or shut down, workers are laid off, and with unpaid workers sales will fall even more, worsening the recession. It almost sounds as if saving is undesirable.

The problem of course is the highly unequal distribution of national wealth and therefore national income, and the fact that the ultra wealthy try to save (and reinvest) most of their large share (given their small numbers,they probably couldn't usefully spend anywhere near all of it anyway). Figure 1 on page 15 shows the approximate distribution of the gross national product in recent years. In a nutshell, the gross national product has been on the order of $14 trillion in recent years, and the distribution of this output has been less than half to the "poorest 90%" of the population, and more than half to the "wealthiest 10%". Instead of spending their large share on the available goods and services, the wealthiest 10% attempts to save and reinvest most of their lions share. As we have repeatedly seen, that is guaranteed to throw the economy into a tailspin within a few years. Which, of course, is exactly what happens over and over and over again. The ultra wealthy income share is large enough to cause serious problems (unused inventory of goods and inadequate investment opportunities). And in the modern global economy, with each business cycle, Laissez Faire Capitalism seems to leave more of our workers on the sidelines in a seemingly permanently impoverished, unemployed and underemployed state.

So it appears that money may not save too well either, at first glance. When we "save for retirement" what we are doing is to fore go a portion of our current consumption by "saving" the money we would otherwise pay for those goods so that the folks who are already retired can buy the goods we passed up, using money they "saved" years ago. A sort of inter generational agreement on money transfers. The goods themselves can't be "stored" for 40 or 50 years, and the match is good enough to avoid serious problems. Social security is exactly this arrangement: when we currently pay tax into social security, we are giving up consumption to those retired folks who buy the goods with their social security checks. Of course, there will be at least a small misfit in the amounts of the funds, which logically should be paid from general taxes to cover a shortage, or shredded in the shredders for a surplus. The "misfit" isn't large enough to cause serious problems, if addressed rationally.

Back to the problem of terribly unequal distribution of the national investment wealth and therefore also of the national income. If you have read the first five chapters of this little book, you already know all about this problem and how it could be fixed.

Duard L. Pruitt   MARCH 2011 - REVISED FEBRUARY 2013

REFERENCES:

(NOTE: To go to the web sites, copy and paste the URLs into your browser. If a URL has changed, try using a search function.)

1.   CLASS-DOMINATION THEORY OF POWER (G. William Domhoff):

http://sociology.ucsc.edu/whorulesamerica/power/wealth.html

http://sociology.ucsc.edu/whorulesamerica/power/wealth.html?2010

2.   WHO RULES AMERICA WEB SITE

http://www.xmarks.com/site/sociology.ucsc.edu/whorulesamerica/power/wealth.html

3.   UNDERSTANDING NEW DEAL TAXATION:

http://www.taxhistory.org/thp/readings.nsf/ArtWeb/1AEBAA68B74ABB918525750C0046BCAF?   OpenDocument

4.   STRIKING IT RICHER:
        http://www.huffingtonpost.com/2009/08/14/income-inequality-is-at-a_n_259516.html

5.   RICH GETTING RICHER:

http://voices.washingtonpost.com/ezraklein/2010/09/the_rich_getting_richer_in_one.html

6.   SAEZ: http://elsa.berkeley.edu/~saez/

7.   GROSS NATIONAL INCOME:

http://siteresources.worldbank.org/DATASTATISTICS/Resources/GNIPC.pdf

8.   ROBERT REICH:
       http://robertreich.org
       http://www.nytimes.com/2010/09/03/opinion/03reich.html?_r=1

9.   HEALTH CARE COST:
       http://www.kaiseredu.org/Issue-Modules/US-Health-Care-
Costs/Background-Brief.aspx

10.   GDP: http://www.forecasts.org/gdp.htm

11.   Social Security cost:
       http://www.ssa.gov/OACT/TRSUM/index.html

12.   Population statistics:
       http://quickfacts.census.gov/qfd/states/00000.html

13.   IRS: http://www.irs.gov/
       http://www.irs.gov/taxstats/article/0,,id=185880,00.html

14.   CENSUS: http://www.census.gov/

http://pubdb3.census.gov/macro/032007/hhinc/new01_001.htm
http://www.census.gov/hhes/www/wealth/2004/wlth04-4.html
       http://quickfacts.census.gov/qfd/states/00000.html

15.   SOCIAL SECURITY
       http://www.ssa.gov/OACT/TRSUM/index.html

16.   WEALTH AND WANT

http://www.wealthandwant.com/issues/income/income_distribution.
html

17.   WIKIPEDIA

http://en.wikipedia.org/wiki/Wealth_in_the_United_States#Distribut
ion_of_wealth

http://en.wikipedia.org/wiki/Personal_income_in_the_United_States

http://en.wikipedia.org/wiki/List_of_countries_by_GNI_(PPP)_per_
capita

18.   STUDENTS OF THE WORLD

http://www.studentsoftheworld.info/infopays/rank/PNBH2.html

19.   WOLFF
       http://www.econ.nyu.edu/user/wolffe/

20.   DOW JONES
       http://www.stockcharts.com/charts/historical/djia1900.html

21.   GNP
       http://www.data360.org/dataset.aspx?Data_Set_Id=353

22.   NATIONAL DEBT

http://www.treasurydirect.gov/govt/reports/pd/histdebt/histdebt.htm

www.ingramcontent.com/pod-product-compliance
Lightning Source LLC
Chambersburg PA
CBHW060227290526
45789CB00003B/1443